AF599275
This book
belongs to:

UNIVERSITY OF CENTRAL ARKANSAS
ALUMNI
ASSOCIATION

DEAR FAMILIES AND FRIENDS,

It is never too early to become part of the UCA family. The UCA Alumni Association has developed this book so you and your family can learn the ABCs of what it means to be a Bear. Each page allows you to explore the many incredible opportunities and resources available on our campus.

This beautifully illustrated book features our beloved school mascots, Sugar Bear and Bruce D. Bear, who will take you on a journey throughout the campus and across time. I hope you enjoy this book and will visit our campus in person to experience all we have to offer. UCA delivers more than you ever imagined, from A to Z, and we want you to be a part of our special, growing community.

GO BEARS!

Houston D Davis

HOUSTON DAVIS
UCA PRESIDENT

WWW.MASCOTBOOKS.COM

B IS FOR BEARS: THE UCA ALPHABET

Illustrated by Riley Hancock Matheny

Written by Kimberly Graves, Riley Hancock Matheny, and Alison Taylor

Edited by Jennifer McCune

For more information, please contact:
Mascot Kids, an imprint of Amplify Publishing Group
620 Herndon Parkway, Suite 220
Herndon, VA 20170
info@mascotbooks.com

Library of Congress Control Number: 2024922986

CPSIA Code: PRKF0125A

ISBN-13: 979-8-89138-110-0

Printed in China

B IS FOR BEARS

THE UCA ALPHABET

Presented by
UCA Alumni Association

Illustrated by
Riley Hancock Matheny

A is for **Amphitheater**, an outdoor stage on the UCA campus. Lots of fun performances happen here like concerts with music, plays with awesome characters, and great speeches.

B is for **Bears**, the official mascot of UCA.
We have two mascots, Sugar Bear and Bruce D. Bear.

C is for **Conway**, the city of colleges.

Conway loves its college students, especially UCA Bears.

ST. LOUIS

NASHVILLE

MEMPHIS

BIRMINGHAM

DALLAS/
FT. WORTH

SHREVEPORT

JACKSON

CITY OF COLLEGES

CONWAY

D is for **drums**, like the ones used in the Bear Marching Band. On football game days, you can watch the band marching to the game down Bruce Street. We call it the Bear Walk, and it's super fun to watch.

E is for **Estes Stadium**, where the football field is called the Stripes. It is a one-of-a-kind field because it has purple and gray stripes.

F is for the **Fountain** at Harding Centennial Plaza. It was named after UCA alumni, Rush and Linda Harding. The fountain is a nice place to sit and read, watch and listen to the water, or enjoy time with friends on campus. And it lights up at night!

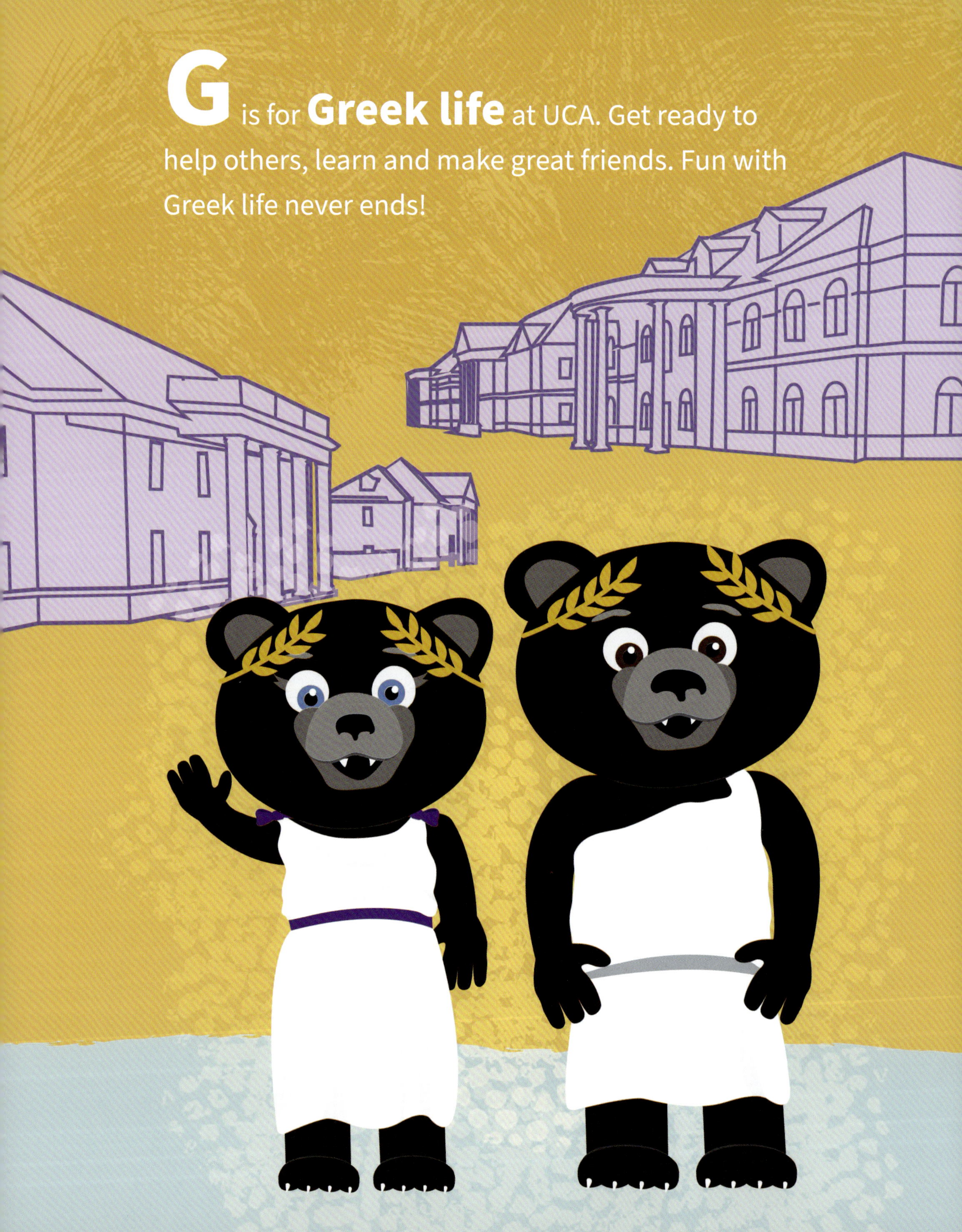
G is for **Greek life** at UCA. Get ready to help others, learn and make great friends. Fun with Greek life never ends!

H is for **Homecoming**, a wonderful week of tradition and fun at UCA. We celebrate our school spirit with all of our Bears and lots of activities, including a big pep rally, the Homecoming football game, and the crowning of the Homecoming King and Queen.

I is for **international**. We love to learn about cultures from all kinds of places. UCA is home to students from all over the world.

J is for **journalism**. We've got great stories to tell! Here, we can learn how to share our stories and take pictures of our Bears doing great things.

K is for **kids' camps** at UCA. Every summer, kids like you can attend many types of camps here. They learn music, science, sports, new languages, and more, and so can you!

L is for the **Legacy Walk**, a path made of special bricks with the names of our graduates and friends. You may find the names of your friends and family here.

M is for **Mudstock**, hosted by the Association of Future Alumni. It is a day of volleyball games played in a big mud pit, which may be a little messy. It's a great time when getting muddy is encouraged!

N is for the **nature reserve**, a place where we learn about bugs, trees, prairies, streams, and all the animals that call it home. It's no wonder that we Bears have a deep love for nature!

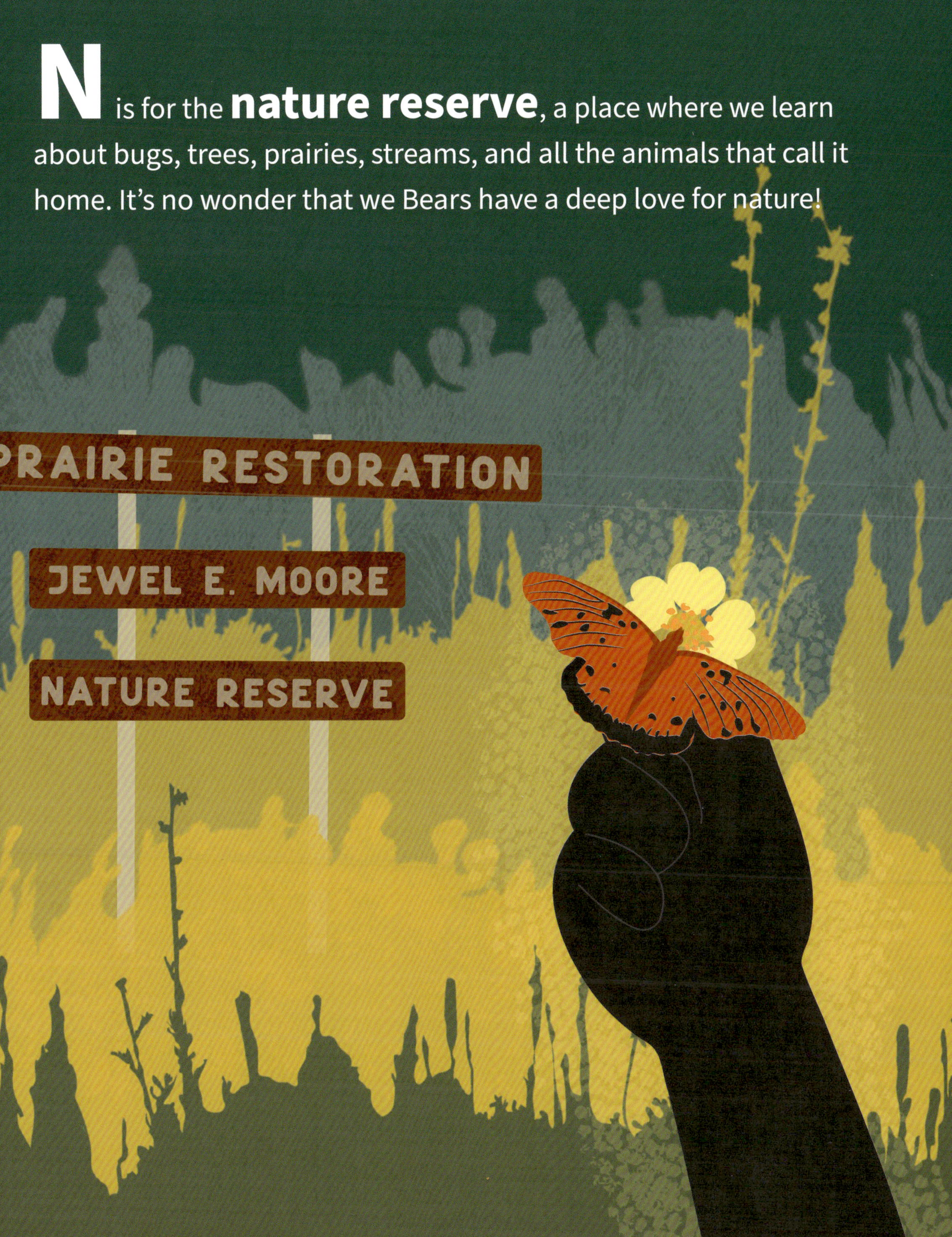

O is for the UCA **Observatory**. It has a giant telescope where you can see planets and stars up close.

P is for **purple and gray**, the official colors of UCA. We wear purple and gray to show our Bear pride.

Q is for **questions**. Our classrooms are full of curious Bears who want to know how things work. Asking questions is a great way to learn.

R is for **reading**. Bears love to read at Torreyson Library. It's full of all kinds of books, computers, collections, and more. Our helpful librarians are there to find just what you need.

S is for **sports**, which is a big part of campus life.

On fields and courts, Bears give their all, in college sports, we stand tall.

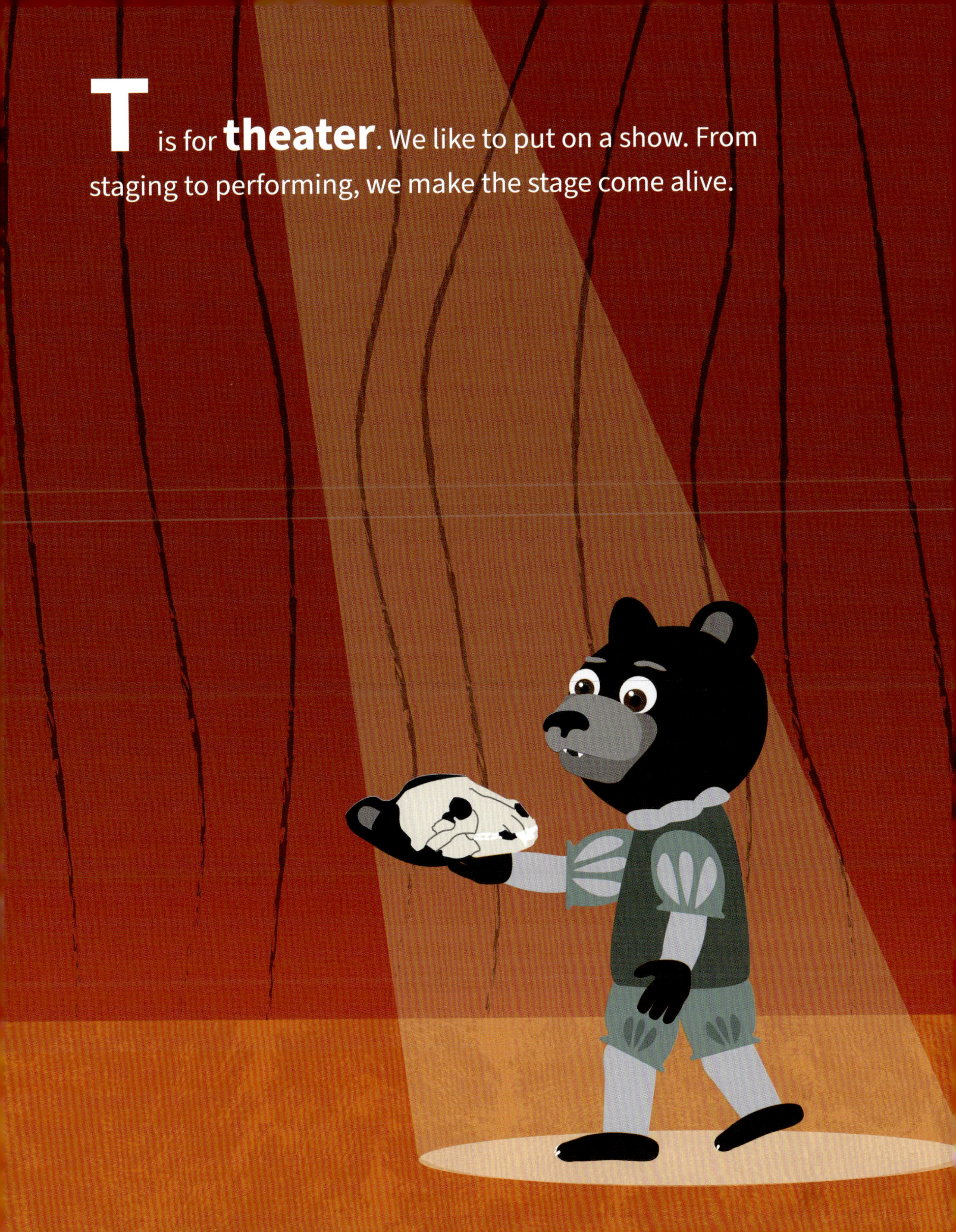

T is for **theater**. We like to put on a show. From staging to performing, we make the stage come alive.

U is for **university**. UCA was started in 1907, so we are over 100 years old! Come and see our oldest building on campus, the Old Main.

V is for **Valor**, a bear sculpture carved from a tree. Valor is in front of Wingo Hall to welcome visitors to campus. Lots of people come to have their picture taken with him!

W is for **Windgate**. The Windgate Center for Fine and Performing Arts is where our Bears learn about and perform music, art, and theater.

X is for **X-ray**. Some of our students learn how to use X-ray machines to see your bones. You can learn too! Many Bears are studying to become nurses, physical therapists, and athletic trainers.

Y is for **you**, a Bear in the making! Whatever your dreams and goals, UCA is here to help you reach your full potential. We can't wait to have you on campus!

Z is for **zoom**. Our Bears like to zig, zag, and zoom around our pretty campus. Whether on bikes, scooters, or skateboards, you can always enjoy hanging out with your friends at UCA.

BACK TO . . .

A is for **alumni**. UCA alumni form a community of graduates and former students who share a common bond and connection to the university. They represent diverse professions and industries but remain united by their shared experiences and memories of UCA. The UCA Alumni Association maintains the connection between UCA alumni and their alma mater. Go Bears!

ONCE A BEAR, ALWAYS A BEAR.

CENTRAL
ARKANSAS

UCA Memories: